PENPALS *for* Handwriting

Intervention Programme
Book 1 – Securing letter formation

Gill Budgell   Kate Ruttle

Supported by the
National Handwriting Association
Promoting good practice

Contents

Scope and sequence

Book 1 – Securing letter formation

1 Letter formation i and l
2 Letter formation j
3 Letter formation t
4 Letter formation u and y
5 Letter formation r
6 Letter formation b
7 Letter formation n
8 Letter formation h
9 Letter formation m
10 Letter formation k
11 Letter formation p
12 Letter formation c
13 Letter formation a
14 Letter formation d
15 Letter formation o
16 Letter formation s
17 Letter formation g
18 Letter formation q
19 Letter formation e
20 Letter formation f
21 Letter formation v and w
22 Letter formation x and z
23 Letter formation A, U, B, D
24 Letter formation C, G, E, F
25 Letter formation J, S, H, K
26 Letter formation I, L, T, M, N
27 Letter formation O, Q, P, R
28 Letter formation V, W, Y, X, Z
29 Numbers 1–10
31 Words and sentences with i
32 Words and sentences with t
33 Words and sentences with u
34 Words and sentences with j
35 Words and sentences with r
36 Words and sentences with b
37 Words and sentences with n
38 Words and sentences with h
39 Words and sentences with m
40 Words and sentences with k
41 Words and sentences with p
42 Words and sentences with c
43 Words and sentences with a
44 Words and sentences with d
45 Words and sentences with o
46 Words and sentences with s
47 Words and sentences with g
48 Words and sentences with q
49 Words and sentences with e
50 Words and sentences with f
51 Words and sentences with v, w and x
52 Words and sentences with y and z

Book 2 – Securing joins

1 Diagonal join to ascender from a
2 Diagonal join to ascender from c
3 Diagonal join to ascender from e
4 Diagonal join to ascender from h and i
5 Diagonal join to ascender from k and l
6 Diagonal join to ascender from m and n
7 Diagonal join to ascender from t and u
8 Diagonal join, no ascender, from a
9 Diagonal join, no ascender, from c and d
10 Diagonal join, no ascender, from e
11 Diagonal join, no ascender, from h and i
12 Diagonal join, no ascender, from k and l
13 Diagonal join, no ascender, from m and n
14 Diagonal join, no ascender, from q
15 Diagonal join, no ascender, from t and u
16 Diagonal join – mixed
17 Diagonal join to an anticlockwise letter from a and c
18 Diagonal join to an anticlockwise letter from d and e
19 Diagonal join to an anticlockwise letter from h and i
20 Diagonal join to an anticlockwise letter from k and l
21 Diagonal join to an anticlockwise letter from m and n
22 Diagonal join to an anticlockwise letter from t and u
23 All diagonal joins (1)
24 All diagonal joins (2)
25 Horizontal join to ascender from o and w
26 Horizontal join, no ascender, from o
27 Horizontal join, no ascender, from v and w
28 Horizontal join to an anticlockwise letter from o
29 Horizontal join to an anticlockwise letter from v and w
30 All horizontal joins
31 Joining to ascender and no ascender from s
32 Joining to an anticlockwise letter from s
33 Joining from b
34 Joining from p
35 Joining to f
36 Joining to and from f
37 Joining to ascender and no ascender from r
38 Joining to an anticlockwise letter from r
39 Practising joined writing (1)
40 Practising joined writing (2)

Book 3 – Securing fluency

1 Keeping closed letters closed – patterns and letter practice
2 Keeping closed letters closed – words
3 Keeping closed letters closed – copying text
4 Keeping closed letters closed – text starter
5 Keeping open letters open – patterns and letter practice
6 Keeping open letters open – words
7 Keeping open letters open – copying text
8 Keeping open letters open – text starter
9 Parallel ascenders and descenders – patterns and letter practice
10 Parallel ascenders and descenders – words
11 Parallel ascenders and descenders – text for copying
12 Parallel ascenders and descenders – text starter
13 Same size x-height letters – patterns and letter practice
14 Same size x-height letters – words
15 Same size x-height letters – text for copying
16 Same size x-height letters – text starter
17 Same height ascenders and capitals – patterns and letter practice
18 Same height ascenders and capitals – words
19 Same height ascenders and capitals – text for copying
20 Same height capitals and ascenders – text starter
21 Keeping ascenders and descenders in proportion – patterns and letter practice
22 Keeping ascenders and descenders in proportion – words
23 Keeping ascenders and descenders in proportion – text for copying
24 Keeping ascenders and descenders in proportion – text starter
25 Regular spaces between letters – patterns and letter practice
26 Regular spaces between letters – words
27 Regular spaces between letters – text for copying
28 Regular spaces between letters – text starter
29 Regular spaces between words – patterns and letter practice
30 Regular spaces between words – words
31 Regular spaces between words – text for copying
32 Regular spaces between words – text starter
33 Regular spaces (all) – patterns and letter practice
34 Regular spaces (all) – words
35 Regular spaces (all) – text for copying
36 Regular spaces (all) – text starter
37 Putting it all together – poem
38 Putting it all together – fiction
39 Putting it all together – instructions
40 Putting it all together – news report

Penpals for Handwriting: Rationale

Even in this technological, computer-literate age, good handwriting remains fundamental to our children's educational achievement. *Penpals for Handwriting* is the only handwriting programme to offer a progression from 3–11 years and it will help you teach children to develop fast, fluent and legible handwriting.

Traditional principles in the contemporary classroom

We believe that:

1. A flexible, fluent and legible handwriting style empowers children to write with confidence and creativity. This entitlement needs careful progression and skilful, discrete teaching that is frequent and continues beyond the initial foundation stages. The earlier that difficulties can be identified, the easier it is to correct them. The promotion of good handwriting skills is dependent on the quality of the teaching.

2. Handwriting is a developmental process with its own distinctive stages of sequential growth. We have identified five stages that form the basic organisational structure of *Penpals*:

   (i) Physical preparation for handwriting: gross and fine motor skills leading to mark-making, patterns and letter formation (Foundation, 3–5 years)

   (ii) Securing correct letter formation (Key Stage 1, 5–6 years)

   (iii) Beginning to join, along with a focus on relative size and spacing (Key Stage 1, 6–7 years)

   (iv) Securing the joins, along with a focus on break letters, legibility, consistency and quality (Lower Key Stage 2, 7–9 years)

   (v) Practising speed, fluency and developing a personalised style for different purposes (Upper Key Stage 2, 9–11 years)

3. Handwriting must also be practised discretely and in context. Beyond the initial foundation stages, *Penpals* provides interactive content with Teacher's Books, Interactives and Practice Books, as well as Workbooks for handwriting practice in the context of age-appropriate spelling, punctuation and grammar. Learning to associate the kinaesthetic handwriting movement with the visual letter pattern and the aural phonemes will help children with learning to spell. However, *Penpals* always takes a 'handwriting first' approach.

4. Choosing the writing implement best suited to the task is an important part of a handwriting education.

Differentiation and intervention

In spite of high-quality teaching, some children find handwriting difficult and laborious. The *Penpals for Handwriting Intervention Programme* (*Penpals Intervention*) helps you to support these children. *Penpals Intervention* is split into three books:

- *Securing letter formation*: which is intended primarily for children from Year 1 to the end of primary school
- *Securing joins*: which is intended primarily for children from Year 3 to the end of primary school and into secondary school
- *Securing fluency*: which is intended primarily for children from Year 5 until the end of Year 9.

The three books all revisit skills which have been taught previously but which have not transferred into the children's curriculum handwriting. It is not appropriate to use each book with children who are younger than the identified age group for that book because the skills will not yet have been introduced and practised through the main *Penpals* resources.

These books do not replace high-quality whole-class teaching using the main *Penpals* resources, but can be used for reinforcement or for individual or small group intervention. However, these intervention materials can also be used in schools which do not have *Penpals* as their main handwriting scheme if:

- children have already been introduced to the letter or join in question **and**
- the handwriting style children have been taught is similar to *Penpals* **and**
- the adult supporting the intervention is able to use familiar language to talk about the unit focus.

Penpals for Handwriting Intervention Programme

High-quality teaching will use *Penpals for Handwriting* to teach and apply the new letters or joins and will then use curriculum opportunities for practice. It is important that, once letter formation or joining has been introduced, it is used in all contexts except informal note taking. Children need to know that 'good handwriting' is not something that is only done in handwriting lessons. In addition, it is easier and quicker to teach good pencil grip, posture and formation from the beginning than it is to correct them later on if they have not been used in all situations.

Penpals Intervention is a series of developmentally structured worksheets which introduce letters and the main join types in the same order as the main *Penpals* programme. However, *Penpals Intervention* may present letter combinations within each join type in a different order from the main programme.

While each worksheet can be used as a standalone, it is preferable to use them alongside the relevant unit from the *Penpals Interactives* so that each letter or join can be watched in animated form and then modelled and practised electronically before children begin the worksheet.

The photocopiable activities on the worksheets can be used and revisited as often as necessary, increasing accuracy and speed on each repetition.

The *Penpals Intervention* books are intended to be used in one of four ways:

- **Quick catch-up:** You can use *Penpals Intervention* as a dip-in resource for children who are new to your class or for those who you think need additional practice with some isolated letters or joins. Use the Contents page to find the best worksheet(s) to address the identified problem and supervise the children while they complete the worksheets to ensure that teaching and learning are focused on progress.
- **Support:** During your whole-class *Penpals* lesson, you may have a few children who are not yet ready for the additional opportunities provided in the Workbook. Those children may benefit from additional handwriting practice which can be afforded by the *Penpals Intervention* worksheets. Please note, however, that there is not a unit-to-unit correspondence and some units may be supported by more than one worksheet whereas others may not have any.
- **Reinforcement:** For some children, a few aspects of handwriting need to be reinforced and secured. In these instances, small-group targeted activities from *Penpals Intervention* can be given for reinforcement, supported by an adult.
- **Intervention:** A few children struggle to learn handwriting. Although this may be linked to an identified special need, for most children it is more likely that their muscles were insufficiently developed when handwriting was first introduced so they are constantly playing 'catch-up' and are not ready to move on with their class. The impact of this increases incrementally as children get older. These children will benefit from a more comprehensive one-to-one or small group intervention, supported by an adult.

A few words from the experts

Handwriting is the ultimate fine motor task, which additionally requires skills in hand–eye co-ordination, organisation and sequencing. We expect these skills of very young children, all too often before they are developmentally ready, for example requiring fine motor control of fingers before having postural stability. Pre-writing skills can be learnt, but we should not expect letter and number formation until they can master an oblique cross (X), which requires crossing midline.

Many children with handwriting difficulties are referred to occupational therapists who can help improve letter formation, fluency and pencil grip, for example, but it would be of greater benefit to make sure children get the basics of handwriting correct at the outset. *Penpals for Handwriting* will help establish the right skills at the right time for each child and so make this essential communication tool a pleasure rather than a chore.

Catherine Elsey, Paediatric Occupational Therapist, National Handwriting Association

How to use *Penpals for Handwriting Intervention* Book 1

Before starting work on any intervention or a programme of additional support, it is essential to assess the child's strengths and difficulties during handwriting lessons and in their other curriculum writing. Support for pre- and post-intervention assessment can be found on pages 11–12.

All the worksheets in this book focus on securing letter formation. They are A5 size so that children have the opportunity to experience quick success followed by the opportunity to move on to a more demanding activity. Alternatively, children can be asked to repeat the same short worksheet activity to improve their performance. The format of each group of worksheets is consistent and predictable so that children can concentrate on the unit focus rather than worrying about learning a new activity. As in any other teaching scenario, the adult may need to motivate the learner or group with specific praise for effort and identified improvements in the unit focus.

For each intervention session:
1. Identify the handwriting focus that needs attention.
2. Select the appropriate worksheet (see the Contents page).
3. Before you begin, read the success criteria from the Checklist at the bottom of the worksheet so children know what is expected of them.

Units 1–22: Lower case letters

These A5 worksheets are presented in two different formats, Worksheet a or b, which you can choose depending on the age and stage of the children.

Only the target letter is traced and written on these sheets.

Worksheet a:
For younger children, aged 5–7, or beginners

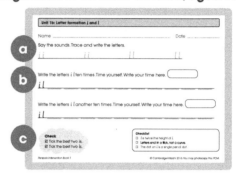

The child completes the worksheet by:

a *Finger tracing while saying the sound.*
Watch children while they do the finger tracing and talk about the key features of each letter (see the Checklist).

b *Writing the letter shape within the hollow letter.*
Children can write inside each letter shape several times.

c *Tracing the letter while saying the sound.*
Now each letter should be traced only once, thereby creating a 'clean' letter shape.

d *Writing the letter while saying the sound.*
This should be completed independently.

e *Self-assessing using the prompts in the Check.*
Encourage children to look at the letter models and to self-assess.

Worksheet b:
For progression or for older children, aged 7+

The child completes the worksheet by:

a *Tracing and writing the letter while saying the sound.*

b *Writing the letter ten times (or as many times as they can in 30 seconds) while saying the sound.*
This activity should be timed to encourage repetition and develop automaticity.

c *Self-assessing using the prompts in the Check.*
Ask children to identify the best letter or letters.

TIPS

- Key features of each letter (e.g. starting point, direction of letter formation and orientation) can be found in the Checklist on each worksheet. See also the *Penpals* letter patters in *Penpals F2 Teacher's Book*.
- Kinaesthetic feedback can, for some children, be enhanced by completing the exercise with their eyes closed to allow them to focus on the movement.
- If finger tracing seems to be insufficient movement for learning, an alternative approach is to trace huge letters with whole arm movements while saying the *Penpals* letter patter.
- Throughout these activities, it is helpful to reinforce the sound represented by the letter. This helps children to create multi-sensory pathways (visual, kinaesthetic and auditory) which support phonics, spelling and handwriting development.
- If children are not yet ready to write the letters independently, revisit the *Penpals F1 Teacher's Book* and Interactives (for gross and fine motor skill development and letter formation) and the *Penpals Workbooks* for F2 (fine motor pattern practice and letter formation practice) or allow them to revisit the worksheets to repeat the tracing activities as often as necessary until they are motor-skill ready.
- For additional practice to reinforce and consolidate the letter formation, use Worksheet b and ask children to trace and say the sounds. Then challenge them either to write the same number of repetitions of the letter more quickly, or to write more repetitions of the letter in a shorter time.

Units 23–28: Capital letters

Letter formation is less critical with capital letters since they are neither joined to nor joined from. However, in *Penpals* we recommend that children write capitals from top to bottom and from left to right.

Each A5 worksheet provides practice of two or three letters which are grouped by shape.

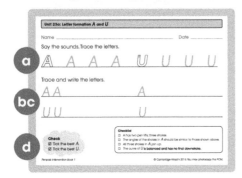

The child completes the worksheet by:

a *Tracing inside each capital letter once.*
   Younger children can finger trace the hollow letter and fill it with colours. Older children should be challenged not to go over the tramlines as they create the letter shape. For all children, point out the starting point and direction-of-travel arrow.

b *Tracing over the capital letters.*
   Encourage older children to trace as accurately as possible, while maintaining a reasonable speed.

c *Tracing and writing the letters.*
   This should be completed independently. You may wish to challenge older children to see how many capitals they can write within a certain time. This creates motivation and a point of comparison if the child repeats the worksheet at a later date.

d *Self-assessing* to identify the best letter or letters. Ask children to use the Check to identify the letter or letters that fit the criteria on the Checklist.

Unit 29 Forming numerals

Both A5 worksheets should be completed by all children who need to revisit formation of numerals from 1–10.

For both Worksheets a and b, the child completes the worksheet by:

a *Tracing/finger tracing a hollow numeral.*
   Younger children can finger trace the hollow number and fill it with colours. Older children should be challenged not to go over the tramlines as they create the numeral. For all children, point out the starting point and direction-of-travel arrow.

b *Tracing over the numerals.*
   Encourage older children to trace as accurately as possible, while maintaining a reasonable speed.

c *Writing the numerals.*
   This should be completed independently.

d *Self-assessing.*
   Ask children to identify their best numerals and ones that still need practice.

Units 30–52: Alliterative words and sentences

Once children have experienced writing all of the lower case letters, they should be sufficiently proficient to trace and copy them.

Worksheet a focuses on words in isolation while Worksheet b shows the words in a sentence for children to trace and write.

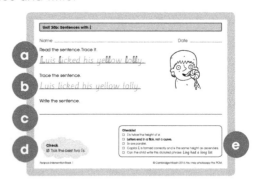

The child completes the worksheet by:

a *Reading and tracing the word or sentence.*
   Before they trace and copy a word or sentence, ensure children understand what they are writing.

b *Tracing the word or sentence.*
   Encourage all children to trace as fluently as possible: it is more important to be fluent than to trace every single letter entirely accurately. Be alert for letters which are not correctly formed in order to identify next steps.

c *Writing the word or sentence.*
   Children should independently copy the word or sentence.

d *Self assessing.*
   Ask children to identify their best word which includes the target letter.

e *Writing the dictated sentence.* (Worksheet b only)
   Draw a baseline on the reverse of the worksheet and then read the sentence slowly while children write it. You can ask children to self-assess their whole sentence and to identify the best version of the target letter.

Handwriting hints: posture and pencil grip

Posture

Good handwriting begins with both feet firmly on the floor so that the downward pressure of the act of writing is balanced evenly between both sides of the body (hips, legs and feet). All the core muscles in the body are necessary if the child is to stay upright and the muscles in the shoulder, arm, wrist, hand and fingers are needed to provide stability and flexibility. In addition, the muscles of the neck are involved to ensure there is no undue discomfort to distract children from their writing.

In order to enable the child to maintain core stability and thus the stability of shoulder, arm, elbow, wrist, hand and fingers, it is important to consider how the child is sitting. If children are sitting with their legs curled up under them or if they are slumped over their work, look at the height of the desk – is it too high or too low for them?

The ideal posture for handwriting is for the child to be seated with their feet flat on the floor and their bottom at the back of the seat so that their lower back is supported by the back of the chair. From this position, they should be able to achieve good balance and maintain the core stability upon which all of the other muscles rely.

From that position, encourage children to lean the upper body forwards slightly when they work. This allows them to stabilise their arms and wrists and to rest the outer edge of their hand lightly on the table. The other hand should rest on the table to ensure that the bodyweight is evenly balanced. This hand is often used to hold the paper securely.

Few children work best when the paper is centred directly in front of them as this pushes their elbow into their body and restricts the movement of their wrist and fingers. Let children experiment with the amount of slope which is best for them: right-handers tend to need to slope their paper with a slight lean to the left, so they are writing slightly 'uphill', whereas left-handers may need a steeper slope to the right so they are writing 'downhill'. This allows them to see what they have written.

Are your elbows off the desk?

Sit up and lean slightly forward

Is your body a fist width away from the desk?

Are your feet flat on the floor?

Are all chair legs touching the ground?

See the posture poster from the *Penpals Poster Pack*.

Pencil grip

The traditional tripod pencil grip – where the pencil is held loosely between the thumb and forefinger, with the middle finger acting as a stabiliser – is the ideal grip (see the *Penpals Poster Pack* and education. cambridge.org/Penpals). This is the most flexible grip for both left- and right-handed writers and is most likely to enable fast, fluent and sustained writing. Using adaptive grips or ergonomic writing tools and making sure the wrist is stable and the grip is not too tight will help most children to develop a comfortable handwriting grip, if used consistently.

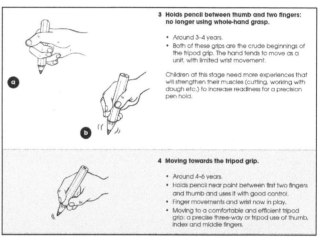

3 Holds pencil between thumb and two fingers: no longer using whole-hand grasp.

- Around 3–4 years.
- Both of these grips are the crude beginnings of the tripod grip. The hand tends to move as a unit, with limited wrist movement.

Children at this stage need more experiences that will strengthen their muscles (cutting, working with dough etc.) to increase readiness for a precision pen hold.

a

b

4 Moving towards the tripod grip.

- Around 4–6 years.
- Holds pencil near point between first two fingers and thumb and uses it with good control.
- Finger movements and wrist now in play.
- Moving to a comfortable and efficient tripod grip: a precise three-way or tripod use of thumb, index and middle fingers.

See the pencil hold poster from the *Penpals Poster Pack*.

If children complain of pain when they write, look carefully at the forefinger with which they hold the pencil: both joints should be bent up in the same direction, creating a rough circle between thumb and forefinger. If the first joint of the forefinger is bent down, the child's pencil grip will be too tight with limited flexibility of the fingers. In that position, the movement comes mostly from the hand, wrist and elbow and great tension is placed on the tendons leading down the back of the hand. It is also important to look carefully at wrist position and stability. Hooking the wrist and lifting the wrist away from the table are both likely to impact overall comfort when writing. Time spent correcting these pencil grip difficulties will be time well spent.

Where a less-than-perfect handwriting grip is established but does not cause the writer pain or fatigue and the writing is of average speed and legible, it will be more beneficial to focus on the content of the writing rather than working on optimising the grip.

Alternative grip

If children find it hard to correct a habitual bad grip, offer them an alternative grip. Ask them to place the pencil between the index and middle fingers and direct the movement of the pencil using thumb, index and middle fingers. This grip is sufficiently flexible to enable fluent, pain-free handwriting when bad habits are too entrenched to change.

Handwriting hints: developing fine motor skills

Writing readiness

'Writing readiness' is a much debated area, but most teachers and occupational therapists believe that, in order to be ready to write, a child:

- should be able to grasp a pencil with fingers rather than the whole hand
- can listen to class and group instructions
- can sustain attention on an adult-initiated activity for about 15 minutes, which should be long enough to complete a *Penpals Intervention* session at this stage
- should be able to draw vertical and horizontal lines and rough circles
- should recognise letter shapes even if they do not know which sound the letter represents
- should have some control over where on a page they place their pencil
- needs to understand and apply vocabulary such as 'top', 'bottom', 'down', 'up', 'across' and 'round' when working on a horizontal piece of paper
- has memory skills to help them recall formation
- should be able to match letters and other simple shapes.

Developing writing readiness

Many of these skills can be developed through activities the children are more likely to perceive as 'fun', such as:

- learning clapping games and finger rhymes
- cooking experiences (e.g. helping to make homemade playdough) that will allow them to knead, roll, press, grate or cut different textures and foods which need different amounts of pressure

- threading or sewing activities
- posting increasingly smaller objects through increasingly smaller gaps (e.g. sorting coins into money boxes, pushing lolly sticks into slits cut into a plastic lid or poking cotton buds / raw spaghetti through the holes of a colander)

- creative activities which involve cutting with different amounts of pressure, measuring objects against other objects, folding paper, making glue dots and placing objects carefully on them
- mark-making activities which involve finer mark-making tools
- construction toys with nuts and bolts or other connections which build finger strength and accuracy
- activities which encourage a 'pincer grip' (e.g. turning coins over, playing tiddlywinks, screwing and unscrewing nuts and bolts, picking up small objects with fingers or tweezers)
- tracing and colouring increasingly complex shapes
- developing cutting skills by cutting straight lines, curved lines, hoops and loops, straight lines with corners, spiky lines, squares, circles, triangles, spirals and then by cutting out shapes that are drawn inside bigger shapes
- playing commercial board games such as Pick-up-Sticks, Operation™, Buckaroo™, Time Shock™, Jenga™ and Kerplunk™, which all require a delicate touch
- playing card games or Top Trumps™, in which children have to hold cards in their hands and select cards
- throwing, catching and twirling batons or making flowing shapes with silky scarves or ribbon sticks
- games which involve making balls move through mazes or placing a card with a maze drawn on it between two small magnets and using the magnet on one side of the card to move the one on its other side through the maze.

Penpals for Handwriting F1: Creative mark-making has many more suggestions for appropriate activities, although you may want to adapt them for use with older children.

Handwriting hints: supporting left-handed writers

At least ten per cent of the population are left-handed. Being left-handed should not be used as an excuse for poor handwriting: with appropriate support, left-handed children have the same capacity for efficient and fluent handwriting as their right-handed peers. However, it is important to remember that teaching left-handed children to write does not simply involve asking them to mirror what right-handed children are doing. The four most important things to be aware of are:

- the position of the exercise book or paper
- the position of the arm and the wrist
- the pencil grip
- the ability to visually monitor the pencil point.

Unless these are considered, many left-handed people adopt a writing position in which they hook their hand around and above the line of text. This is cramped, uncomfortable and difficult to sustain for any length of time.

Left-handed children will particularly benefit from large-scale mark-making activities using chalk, marker pens, paint-brushes, fingers, sticks and so on (see *Penpals F1 Teacher's Book*). These children may need to have access to these activities for longer than their right-handed peers while they learn to make letter shapes using big, whole-arm motions.

The position of the exercise book or paper relative to the position of the arm and the wrist

Right-handed children *pull* the pencil across the paper from left to right so they can always see what they have written. Left-handed children *push* the pencil across the paper from left to right so their hand tends to cover up their writing. In order to avoid this, left-handed writers need to tilt their books at a more acute angle than right-handed writers.

Left-handed children should place the paper to the left of their midline and slope the paper so that they are writing 'downhill' towards themselves, without covering what they have just written.

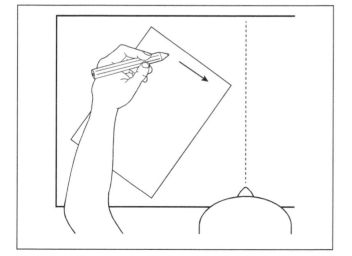

- Ask these children to place their arm on the table in the position they use to write.
- Line up the vertical edges of their paper to be parallel with their forearm, and then slightly increase the slope.

The 'correct' angle will be different for all children, and some may even prefer not to have a tilted page; but teaching them with this level of tilted page from the beginning will help them to become accustomed to it. Ensure that the hand which stabilises the paper is below where the children are writing, or is well above it as the writer moves towards the bottom of the page.

Pencil grip

Whereas right-handed children will often hold their pencil at about 1-1.5 cm from the point, left-handed children should be encouraged to hold the pencil slightly further from the point so that they can see what they have written. You may wish to place a soft pencil grip at this distance from the point until the child automatically holds the pencil at this distance.

The tripod pencil grip (see the *Penpals Poster Pack* and education.cambridge.org/Penpals) is the most flexible grip for both left- and right-handed writers and is most likely to enable fast, fluent and sustained writing. The alternative grip described on page 7 is equally appropriate for left-handed children.

Handwriting hints: using pencil grips, ergonomic pencils and writing slopes

Various pencil grips are available to meet a range of difficulties. So, before you prescribe a generic pencil grip, consider what the problem is and how old the child is, since as they get older some children become embarrassed by using pencil grips.

Improving the grip

Improving the tripod grip is the most common reason for offering a child a pencil grip. A range of options are available.

- The most traditional pencil grip is a triangular prism-shape which you push onto a pencil. Many children find it hard to sustain writing with these grips as they are not shaped to accommodate fingers.

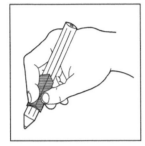

- More ergonomic grips are often shaped around fingers and also allow for the different needs of left- and right-handed children. These grips are often softer to relieve tension and fatigue while reinforcing a good tripod grip. These grips often come with 'wings' to prevent fingers and thumbs from overlapping and crossing over each other.

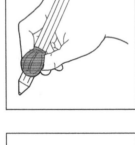

- The writing 'claw', which is a grip with three horizontal cups to accommodate finger tips, is good for supporting younger children who are just discovering a tripod grip.

Relieving tension and providing sensory feedback

For slightly older children, there are a range of textured and padded grips that can both reduce strain if children are holding the pencil too tightly and give increased control to children who benefit from clear sensory feedback.

As we write, our hands tend to slip down the barrel of the writing instrument, causing us to grip harder, which in turn puts pressure on the tendons in the hand. Grips can be used to reduce the slippage.

- Soft grips, which are made from tubes of foam or silicon, can help to relieve tension and fatigue caused by gripping a pencil too tightly. These are ideal for older children whose pencil grip is broadly adequate but whose hands get tired writing.
- Textured grips, which are usually made from gel or silicone tubes, give particular support to children who need tactile feedback. These can be slightly shaped to stabilise fingers.

Ergonomic pencils

In addition to pencil grips, which can be transferred to different writing and colouring implements, you can now buy ergonomic pens and pencils. At the simplest level, these are simply triangular shaped to encourage the use of a tripod grip. However, most of these writing implements are now moulded to encourage the correct grip. Many brands also supply various designs to accommodate different-sized hands and the different stages children progress through as they develop an automatic and comfortable tripod grip.

Writing slopes

Some children benefit from using a writing slope or board because the use of the slope reduces strain on the neck, back, shoulders and eyes. If a child is experiencing any difficulties with writing, it is worth exploring the use of a writing slope. Ideally, buy one with a non-slip surface or put a non-slip cover onto the slope. You may also need a non-slip cover on the desk or table where the child will be sitting to ensure that the slope stays still.

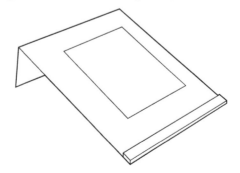

Writing slopes are particularly useful for:

- left-handed children
- children with dyslexia
- children with a developmental co-ordination disorder (DCD)/dyspraxia.

Teacher assessment sheet

Name .... Date ....

Intervention dates: .... Letter(s) focused on during intervention: ....

Look at letter formation in isolation, in words and sentences during handwriting sessions and in the child's writing book and cross-curricular writing. Record the date at which letter formation is first seen to be spontaneously accurate and then the date on which it is secure.

Letter	In isolation	In sentences	In curriculum writing
a			
b			
c			
d			
e			
f			
g			
h			
i			
j			
k			
l			
m			
n			
o			
p			
q			
r			
s			
t			
u			
v			
w			
x			
y			
z			

Child assessment sheet

Name .... Date ....

Before the intervention

I am good at writing these letters:

_____

I sometimes need help with these letters:

_____

After the intervention

Letters	My self-assessment is:	My comments are:
	1 2 3	
	1 2 3	
	1 2 3	
	1 2 3	
	1 2 3	
	1 2 3	
	1 2 3	
	1 2 3	

Next, I want to improve my handwriting by:

_____

_____

_____

Name .... Date ....

Finger trace. Say the sounds. Write inside the letters.

Say the sounds. Trace the letters.

Say the sounds. Write the letters.

i   *l*

Check
☑ Tick the best *i*
☑ Tick the best *l*.

Checklist
☐ *l* is twice the height of *i*.
☐ Letters end in a flick, not a curve.
☐ The dot on *i* is a single pencil dot.

Name .... Date ....

Say the sounds. Trace and write the letters.

Write the letters *i l* ten times. Time yourself. Write your time here. ⬭

i l

Write the letters *i l* another ten times. Time yourself. Write your time here. ⬭

i l

Check
☑ Tick the best two *i*s.
☑ Tick the best two *l*s.

Checklist
☐ *l* is twice the height of *i*.
☐ Letters end in a flick, not a curve.
☐ The dot on *i* is a single pencil dot.

Name .... Date ....

Finger trace. Say the sound. Write inside the letters.

Say the sound. Trace the letters.

Say the sound. Write the letter.

j

Check
☑ Tick the best *j*.

Checklist
☐ The bottom of the letter curves to the left.
☐ The curve is formed without a hook.
☐ The top of the *j* is the same height as a letter *i*.

Penpals Intervention Book 1

Name .... Date ....

Say the sound. Trace and write the letters.

Write the letter *j* ten times. Time yourself. Write your time here.

j

Write the letter *j* another ten times. Time yourself. Write your time here.

j

Check
☑ Tick the best two *j*s.

Checklist
☐ The bottom of the letter curves to the left.
☐ The curve is formed without a hook.
☐ The top of the *j* is the same height as a letter *i*.

Penpals Intervention Book 1

Unit 3a: Letter formation *t*

Name .... Date ....

Finger trace. Say the sound. Write inside the letters.

t t t t t t t

Say the sound. Trace the letters.

tt tt tt tt tt tt tt tt

Say the sound. Write the letter.

t

Check
☑ Tick the best *t*.

Checklist
☐ The bottom of the letter ends in a curve, not a flick.
☐ The cross bar is placed towards the top of the downstroke.
☐ *t* is slightly shorter than *h*.

Penpals Intervention Book 1

© Cambridge-Hitachi 2016. You may photocopy this PCM.

Unit 3b: Letter formation *t*

Name .... Date ....

Say the sound. Trace and write the letters.

tt   tt   tt   tt

Write the letter *t* ten times. Time yourself. Write your time here. ⬭

t

Write the letter *t* another ten times. Time yourself. Write your time here. ⬭

t

Check
☑ Tick the best two *t*s.

Checklist
☐ The bottom of the letter ends in a curve, not a flick.
☐ The cross bar is placed towards the top of the downstroke.
☐ *t* is slightly shorter than *h*.

Penpals Intervention Book 1

© Cambridge-Hitachi 2016. You may photocopy this PCM.

Name .... Date ....

Finger trace. Say the sounds. Write inside the letters.

u   u   u   y   y   y

Say the sounds. Trace the letters.

u u   u u   u u   y y   y y   y y

Say the sounds. Write the letters.

u _____   y _____

Check
☑ Tick the best u.
☑ Tick the best y.

Checklist
☐ The downstroke traces the line of the upstroke.
☐ Downstrokes and upstrokes have equal heights.
☐ The length of the tail of the y matches the height above the line.

Name .... Date ....

Say the sounds. Trace and write the letters.

u y   u y   u y   u y   u y   u y   u y   u y

Write the letters u y ten times. Time yourself. Write your time here. ⬭

u y _____ _____ _____ _____ _____ _____ _____

Write the letters u y another ten times. Time yourself. Write your time here. ⬭

u y _____ _____ _____ _____ _____ _____ _____

Check
☑ Tick the best two u s.
☑ Tick the best two y s.

Checklist
☐ The downstroke traces the line of the upstroke.
☐ Downstrokes and upstrokes have equal heights.
☐ The length of the tail of the y matches the height above the line.

Name .... Date ....

Finger trace. Say the sound. Write inside the letters.

r   r   r   r   r   r   r

Say the sound. Trace the letters.

rr   rr   rr   rr   rr   rr   rr   rr

Say the sound. Write the letter.

r

Check
☑ Tick the best *r*.

Checklist
☐ The letter starts at the top.
☐ The bounce-up stroke traces the same line as the downstroke.
☐ The short curve stops at about 1 o'clock.

Name .... Date ....

Say the sound. Trace and write the letters.

rr   rr   rr   rr

Write the letter *r* ten times. Time yourself. Write your time here. ⬭

r

Write the letter *r* another ten times. Time yourself. Write your time here. ⬭

r

Check
☑ Tick the best two *r* s.

Checklist
☐ The letter starts at the top.
☐ The bounce-up stroke traces the same line as the downstroke.
☐ The short curve stops at about 1 o'clock.

Unit 6a: Letter formation *b*

Name .... Date ....

Finger trace. Say the sound. Write inside the letters.

b b b b b b b

Say the sound. Trace the letters.

b b   b b   b b   b b   b b   b b

Say the sound. Write the letter.

b

Check
☑ Tick the best *b*.

Checklist
☐ The letter starts at the top.
☐ The bounce-up stroke traces the same line as the downstroke.
☐ The letter is fully closed at the bottom.

Unit 6b: Letter formation *b*

Name .... Date ....

Say the sound. Trace and write the letters.

b b   b b   b b   b b

Write the letter *b* ten times. Time yourself. Write your time here. (   )

b ____ ____ ____ ____ ____ ____ ____ ____ ____ ____

Write the letter *b* another ten times. Time yourself. Write your time here. (   )

b ____ ____ ____ ____ ____ ____ ____ ____ ____ ____

Check
☑ Tick the best two *b*s.

Checklist
☐ The letter starts at the top.
☐ The bounce-up stroke traces the same line as the downstroke.
☐ The letter is fully closed at the bottom.

Name .... Date ....

Finger trace. Say the sound. Write inside the letters.

n   n   n   n   n   n

Say the sound. Trace the letters.

nn   nn   nn   nn   nn   nn

Say the sound. Write the letter.

n _____

Check
☑ Tick the best *n*.

Checklist
☐ The letter starts at the top.
☐ The bounce-up stroke traces the same line as the downstroke.
☐ Downstrokes are parallel.

Name .... Date ....

Say the sound. Trace and write the letters.

nn   nn   nn   nn _____

Write the letter *n* ten times. Time yourself. Write your time here. ⬭

n _____

Write the letter *n* another ten times. Time yourself. Write your time here. ⬭

n _____

Check
☑ Tick the best two *n*s.

Checklist
☐ The letter starts at the top.
☐ The bounce-up stroke traces the same line as the downstroke.
☐ Downstrokes are parallel.

Unit 8a: Letter formation *h*

Name .... Date ....

Finger trace. Say the sound. Write inside the letters.

h h h h h h h

Say the sound. Trace the letters.

h h   h h   h h   h h   h h   h h

Say the sound. Write the letter.

h _____

Check
☑ Tick the best *h*.

Checklist
☐ The letter starts at the top.
☐ The downstroke is twice the height of the bounce-up stroke.
☐ The second downstroke is parallel to the first.

Penpals Intervention Book 1   © Cambridge-Hitachi 2016. You may photocopy this PCM.

Unit 8b: Letter formation *h*

Name .... Date ....

Say the sound. Trace and write the letters.

h h   h h   h h   h h _____

Write the letter *h* ten times. Time yourself. Write your time here. ⬭

h _____

Write the letter *h* another ten times. Time yourself. Write your time here. ⬭

h _____

Check
☑ Tick the best two *h*s.

Checklist
☐ The letter starts at the top.
☐ The downstroke is twice the height of the bounce-up stroke.
☐ The second downstroke is parallel to the first.

Penpals Intervention Book 1   © Cambridge-Hitachi 2016. You may photocopy this PCM.

Name .... Date ....

Finger trace. Say the sound. Write inside the letters.

m   m   m   m   m

Say the sound. Trace the letters.

m m   m m   m m   m m

Say the sound. Write the letter.

m

Check
☑ Tick the best ***m***.

Checklist
☐ The letter starts at the top.
☐ The bounce-up strokes trace the same line as the downstrokes.
☐ Both curves are the same height.

Unit 9b: Letter formation *m*

Name .... Date ....

Say the sound. Trace and write the letters.

m m   m m   m m   m m

Write the letter ***m*** ten times. Time yourself. Write your time here. ⬭

m

Write the letter ***m*** another ten times. Time yourself. Write your time here. ⬭

m

Check
☑ Tick the best two ***m***s.

Checklist
☐ The letter starts at the top.
☐ The bounce-up strokes trace the same line as the downstrokes.
☐ Both curves are the same height.

Name .... Date ....

Finger trace. Say the sound. Write inside the letters.

k   *k*   *k*   *k*   *k*   *k*

Say the sound. Trace the letters.

k k   *k k*   *k k*   *k k*   *k k*   *k k*

Say the sound. Write the letter.

k _____

Check
☑ Tick the best *k*.

Checklist
☐ The downstroke is twice the height of the bounce-up.
☐ The end of the hoop touches the long downstroke.
☐ The hoop and the final diagonal are the same distance from the downstroke.

Name .... Date ....

Say the sound. Trace and write the letters.

k k   *k k*   *k k*   *k k* _____

Write the letter *k* ten times. Time yourself. Write your time here. ⬭

k _____

Write the letter *k* another ten times. Time yourself. Write your time here. ⬭

k _____

Check
☑ Tick the best two *k* s.

Checklist
☐ The downstroke is twice the height of the bounce-up.
☐ The end of the hoop touches the long downstroke.
☐ The hoop and the final diagonal are the same distance from the downstroke.

Name .... Date ....

Finger trace. Say the sound. Write inside the letters.

p   p   p   p   p   p

Say the sound. Trace the letters.

pp   pp   pp   pp   pp   pp

Say the sound. Write the letter.

p

Check
☑ Tick the best *p*.

Checklist
☐ The letter starts at the top of the downstroke.
☐ The bounce-up traces the same line as the downstroke.
☐ The end of the curve touches the long downstroke and rests on the baseline.

Name .... Date ....

Say the sound. Trace and write the letters.

pp   pp   pp   pp

Write the letter *p* ten times. Time yourself. Write your time here. ⬭

p

Write the letter *p* another ten times. Time yourself. Write your time here. ⬭

p

Check
☑ Tick the best two *p*s.

Checklist
☐ The letter starts at the top of the downstroke.
☐ The bounce-up traces the same line as the downstroke.
☐ The end of the curve touches the long downstroke and rests on the baseline.

Unit 12a: Letter formation *c*

Name .... Date ....

Finger trace. Say the sound. Write inside the letters.

C C C C C C C C

Say the sound. Trace the letters.

c c   c c   c c   c c   c c   c c

Say the sound. Write the letter.

c _____

Check
☑ Tick the best *c*.

Checklist
☐ The letter starts at 1 o'clock.
☐ The curve at the top of the letter matches that at the bottom of the letter.

Penpals Intervention Book 1   © Cambridge-Hitachi 2016. You may photocopy this PCM.

Unit 12b: Letter formation *c*

Name .... Date ....

Say the sound. Trace and write the letters.

c c   c c   c c   c c

Write the letter *c* ten times. Time yourself. Write your time here. ⬚

c _____

Write the letter *c* another ten times. Time yourself. Write your time here. ⬚

c _____

Check
☑ Tick the best two *c*s.

Checklist
☐ The letter starts at 1 o'clock.
☐ The curve at the top of the letter matches that at the bottom of the letter.

Penpals Intervention Book 1   © Cambridge-Hitachi 2016. You may photocopy this PCM.

Unit 13a: Letter formation *a*

Name .... Date ....

Finger trace. Say the sound. Write inside the letters.

a   *a*   *a*   *a*   *a*   *a*

Say the sound. Trace the letters.

a a   *a a*   *a a*   *a a*   *a a*   *a a*

Say the sound. Write the letter.

a

Check

☑ Tick the best *a*.

Checklist

☐ The letter starts at 1 o'clock.
☐ The letter is fully closed at the top.
☐ The downstroke traces the line of the upstroke.

Unit 13b: Letter formation *a*

Name .... Date ....

Say the sound. Trace and write the letters.

a a   *a a*   *a a*   *a a*

Write the letter *a* ten times. Time yourself. Write your time here. ⬭

a

Write the letter *a* another ten times. Time yourself. Write your time here. ⬭

a

Check

☑ Tick the best two *a*s.

Checklist

☐ The letter starts at 1 o'clock.
☐ The letter is fully closed at the top.
☐ The downstroke traces the line of the upstroke.

Name .... Date ....

Finger trace. Say the sound. Write inside the letters.

d d d d d d

Say the sound. Trace the letters.

dd   dd   dd   dd   dd   dd

Say the sound. Write the letter.

d _____

Check
☑ Tick the best *d*.

Checklist
☐ The letter starts at the top of the curve at 1 o'clock.
☐ The curve is joined to the downstroke.
☐ The downstroke traces the line of the upstroke.

Penpals Intervention Book 1   © Cambridge-Hitachi 2016. You may photocopy this PCM.

Name .... Date ....

Say the sound. Trace and write the letters.

dd   dd   dd   dd

Write the letter *d* ten times. Time yourself. Write your time here.

d _____

Write the letter *d* another ten times. Time yourself. Write your time here.

d _____

Check
☑ Tick the best two *d*s.

Checklist
☐ The letter starts at the top of the curve at 1 o'clock.
☐ The curve is joined to the downstroke.
☐ The downstroke traces the line of the upstroke.

Penpals Intervention Book 1   © Cambridge-Hitachi 2016. You may photocopy this PCM.

Unit 15a: Letter formation o

Name .... Date ....

Finger trace. Say the sound. Write inside the letters.

Ⓞ o   Ⓞ   Ⓞ o   Ⓞ   Ⓞ   Ⓞ

Say the sound. Trace the letters.

O O   O O   O O   O O   O O   O O

Say the sound. Write the letter.

O _____

Check
☑ Tick the best o.

Checklist
☐ The letter starts at 1 o'clock.
☐ The letter is formed anticlockwise.
☐ The letter begins and ends at the same place.

Unit 15b: Letter formation o

Name .... Date ....

Say the sound. Trace and write the letters.

O O   O O   O O   O O

Write the letter o ten times. Time yourself. Write your time here. (_____)

O _____

Write the letter o another ten times. Time yourself. Write your time here. (_____)

O _____

Check
☑ Tick the best two o s.

Checklist
☐ The letter starts at 1 o'clock.
☐ The letter is formed anticlockwise.
☐ The letter begins and ends at the same place.

Unit 16a: Letter formation *s*

Name .... Date ....

Finger trace. Say the sound. Write inside the letters.

S   S   S   S   S   S   S

Say the sound. Trace the letters.

S S   S S   S S   S S   S S   S S   S S   S S

Say the sound. Write the letter.

s _____

Check
☑ Tick the best *s*.

Checklist
☐ The letter begins with a curve.
☐ The curves are balanced.
☐ The letter is the same height as an *a*.

Penpals Intervention Book 1   © Cambridge-Hitachi 2016. You may photocopy this PCM.

Unit 16b: Letter formation *s*

Name .... Date ....

Say the sound. Trace and write the letters.

s s   s s   s s   s s

Write the letter *s* ten times. Time yourself. Write your time here. ⬭

s _____

Write the letter *s* another ten times. Time yourself. Write your time here. ⬭

s _____

Check
☑ Tick the best two *s* s.

Checklist
☐ The letter begins with a curve.
☐ The curves are balanced.
☐ The letter is the same height as an *a*.

Penpals Intervention Book 1   © Cambridge-Hitachi 2016. You may photocopy this PCM.

Unit 17a: Letter formation *g*

Name .... Date ....

Finger trace. Say the sound. Write inside the letters.

g   *g*   *g*   *g*   *g*   *g*

Say the sound. Trace the letters.

gg   *gg*   *gg*   *gg*   *gg*   *gg*

Say the sound. Write the letter.

g _____

Check
☑ Tick the best *g*.

Checklist
☐ The letter starts at 1 o'clock.
☐ The letter is closed at the top of the straight upstroke.
☐ Half of the downstroke hangs beneath the baseline.

Unit 17b: Letter formation *g*

Name .... Date ....

Say the sound. Trace and write the letters.

gg   *gg*   *gg*   *gg*

Write the letter *g* ten times. Time yourself. Write your time here. ⬭

g _____

Write the letter *g* another ten times. Time yourself. Write your time here. ⬭

g _____

Check
☑ Tick the best two *g*s.

Checklist
☐ The letter starts at 1 o'clock.
☐ The letter is closed at the top of the straight upstroke.
☐ Half of the downstroke hangs beneath the baseline.

Name .... Date ....

Finger trace. Say the sound. Write inside the letters.

Say the sound. Trace the letters.

Say the sound. Write the letter.

q

Check
☑ Tick the best q.

Checklist
□ The letter starts at 1 o'clock.
□ The curve of the letter is closed.
□ The flick goes up diagonally towards the baseline but is small.

Penpals Intervention Book 1

Name .... Date ....

Say the sound. Trace and write the letters.

Write the letter q ten times. Time yourself. Write your time here. ⬭

q

Write the letter q another ten times. Time yourself. Write your time here. ⬭

q

Check
☑ Tick the best two q s.

Checklist
□ The letter starts at 1 o'clock.
□ The curve of the letter is closed.
□ The flick goes up diagonally towards the baseline but is small.

Penpals Intervention Book 1

Name .... Date ....

Finger trace. Say the sound. Write inside the letters.

e   e   e   e   e   e

Say the sound. Trace the letters.

ee   ee   ee   ee   ee   ee

Say the sound. Write the letter.

e _____

Check
☑ Tick the best *e*.

Checklist
☐ The letter begins with a gentle curve from left to right.
☐ The starting point and downwards curve should touch.
☐ The curve at the bottom matches that at the top.

Name .... Date ....

Say the sound. Trace and write the letters.

ee   ee   ee   ee _____

Write the letter *e* ten times. Time yourself. Write your time here. ⬭

e _____

Write the letter *e* another ten times. Time yourself. Write your time here. ⬭

e _____

Check
☑ Tick the best two *e*s.

Checklist
☐ The letter begins with a gentle curve from left to right.
☐ The starting point and downwards curve should touch.
☐ The curve at the bottom matches that at the top.

Name _____ Date _____

Finger trace. Say the sound. Write inside the letters.

ff   ff   ff   ff   ff   ff   ff

Say the sound. Trace the letters.

ff   ff   ff   ff   ff   ff   ff   ff

Say the sound. Write the letter.

f _____

Check
☑ Tick the best *f*.

Checklist
☐ The letter starts as a curve from 1 o'clock.
☐ The downstroke is parallel with those in other letters.
☐ The top and bottom curves are similar sizes.
☐ The letter has a horizontal cross bar.

Name _____ Date _____

Say the sound. Trace and write the letters.

ff   ff   ff   ff _____

Write the letter *f* ten times. Time yourself. Write your time here. ⬭

f _ _ _ _ _ _ _ _ _ _ _ _ _ _ _ _ _

Write the letter *f* another ten times. Time yourself. Write your time here. ⬭

f _ _ _ _ _ _ _ _ _ _ _ _ _ _ _ _ _

Check
☑ Tick the best two *f*s.

Checklist
☐ The letter starts as a curve from 1 o'clock.
☐ The downstroke is parallel with those in other letters.
☐ The top and bottom curves are similar sizes.
☐ The letter has a horizontal cross bar.

Name .... Date ....

Finger trace. Say the sounds. Write inside the letters.

V V V W W W

Say the sounds. Trace the letters.

v v   v v   v v   w w   w w   w w

Say the sounds. Write the letters.

V   W

Check
☑ Tick the best *v*.
☑ Tick the best *w*.

Checklist
☐ All sloped downstrokes and upstrokes are the same height.
☐ The letters are the same height.
☐ The 'v's in the *w* are balanced.

Name .... Date ....

Say the sounds. Trace and write the letters.

v w   v w   v w   v w   v w   v w

Write the letters *v w* ten times. Time yourself. Write your time here.

v w

Write the letters *v w* another ten times. Time yourself. Write your time here.

v w

Check
☑ Tick the best two *v*s.
☑ Tick the best two *w*s.

Checklist
☐ All sloped downstrokes and upstrokes are the same height.
☐ The letters are the same height.
☐ The 'v's in the *w* are balanced.

Name .... Date ....

Finger trace. Say the sounds. Write inside the letters.

X X X Z Z Z

Say the sounds. Trace the letters.

XX XX XX   ZZ ZZ ZZ

Say the sounds. Write the letters.

X _____   Z _____

Check
☑ Tick the best x.
☑ Tick the best z.

Checklist
☐ x and z are the same height and the same width.
☐ The cross of x is at, or slightly above, the midpoint.
☐ The slope of z is parallel to the slope of x.

Penpals Intervention Book 1

© Cambridge-Hitachi 2016. You may photocopy this PCM.

Name .... Date ....

Say the sounds. Trace and write the letters.

XZ   XZ   XZ   XZ   XZ   XZ

Write the letters *x z* ten times. Time yourself. Write your time here. ( )

XZ _____

Write the letters *x z* another ten times. Time yourself. Write your time here. ( )

XZ _____

Check
☑ Tick the best two xs.
☑ Tick the best two zs.

Checklist
☐ x and z are the same height and the same width.
☐ The cross of x is at, or slightly above, the midpoint.
☐ The slope of z is parallel to the slope of x.

Penpals Intervention Book 1

© Cambridge-Hitachi 2016. You may photocopy this PCM.

Name .... Date ....

Say the sounds. Trace the letters.

A A A A A U U U U U

Trace and write the letters.

A A   A

U U   U

Check
☑ Tick the best *A*.
☑ Tick the best *U*.

Checklist
☐ *A* has two pen lifts and three strokes.
☐ The angles of the strokes in *A* should be similar to those shown above.
☐ All three strokes in *A* join up.
☐ The curve of *U* is balanced and has no final downstroke.

Name .... Date ....

Say the sounds. Trace the letters.

B B B B D D D D

Trace and write the letters.

B B   B

D D   D

Check
☑ Tick the best *B*.
☑ Tick the best *D*.

Checklist
☐ *B* and *D* each have one pen lift and two strokes.
☐ The downstroke meets the curve(s) at the top and bottom of the letter.
☐ The lower curve of *B* is the same size as, or slightly larger than, the upper curve.

Name .... Date ....

Say the sounds. Trace the letters.

C C C C   G G G G

Trace and write the letters.

C C   C _____

G G   G _____

Check
☑ Tick the best C.
☑ Tick the best G.

Checklist
☐ The letters start at about 1 o'clock.
☐ The top and bottom curves are balanced.
☐ The bar across the G is horizontal.
☐ Lift the pen to form the horizontal bar across the G.

Name .... Date ....

Say the sounds. Trace the letters.

E E E E   F F F F

Trace and write the letters.

E E   E _____

F F   F _____

Check
☑ Tick the best E.
☑ Tick the best F.

Checklist
☐ The horizontal strokes in each letter are parallel.
☐ Write the vertical line and then add each horizontal line after a pen lift.
☐ The top and bottom horizontal strokes of E are the same length.

Name .... Date ....

Say the sounds. Trace the letters.

J J J J J S S S S S

Trace and write the letters.

J J   J

S S   S

Check
☑ Tick the best *J*.
☑ Tick the best *S*.

Checklist
☐ The curve at the bottom of *J* is clear, but not too high.
☐ Lift the pen to form the horizontal bar on the *J*.
☐ The middle portion of the *S* is sloped.
☐ Capital *S* is twice the height of lowercase *s*.

Penpals Intervention Book 1

Name .... Date ....

Say the sounds. Trace the letters.

H H H H H K K K K K

Trace and write the letters.

H H   H

K K   K

Check
☑ Tick the best *H*.
☑ Tick the best *K*.

Checklist
☐ The downstrokes in *H* are similar lengths.
☐ The angles of the slopes in *K* are balanced.
☐ The slopes meet the vertical downstroke of *K* in a sharp point.
☐ *H* has two pen lifts and three strokes; *K* has one pen lift and two strokes.

Penpals Intervention Book 1

Name .... Date ....

Say the sounds. Trace the letters.

I I I I I L L L L T T T T

Trace and write the letters.

II _____ LL _____ TT _____

II _____ LL _____ TT _____

Check
☑ Tick the best *I*.
☑ Tick the best *L*.
☑ Tick the best *T*.

Checklist
☐ *I* has two pen lifts and three strokes; *T* has one pen lift and two strokes.
☐ All horizontal strokes touch the vertical line.
☐ Vertical strokes are all parallel.

Name .... Date ....

Say the sounds. Trace the letters.

M M M M N N N N

Trace and write the letters.

MM _____ M _____

NN _____ N _____

Check
☑ Tick the best *M*.
☑ Tick the best *N*.

Checklist
☐ The angle of slopes should be similar to those shown above.
☐ All strokes meet at sharp points.
☐ Vertical strokes are parallel.
☐ *M* and *N* each have one pen lift and two strokes.

Name .... Date ....

Say the sounds. Trace the letters.

O   O   O   O   Q   Q   Q   Q

Trace and write the letters.

O O ....   O ....

Q Q ....   Q ....

Check
☑ Tick the best O.
☑ Tick the best Q.

Checklist
☐ Letters start at 1 o'clock.
☐ The letters are taller than they are wide.
☐ The tail of the Q is positioned at 5 o'clock.

Name .... Date ....

Say the sounds. Trace the letters.

P   P   P   P   R   R   R   R

Trace and write the letters.

P P ....   P ....

R R ....   R ....

Check
☑ Tick the best P.
☑ Tick the best R.

Checklist
☐ The curve meets the vertical downstroke at the top and halfway down.
☐ The slope of R begins halfway down the vertical downstroke.
☐ The slope of R finishes on the baseline.
☐ P and R each have a pen lift and two strokes.

Name .... Date ....

Say the sounds. Trace the letters.

V V V W W W Y Y Y

Trace and write the letters.

V V   W W   Y Y

V V   W W   Y Y

Check
☑ Tick the best V.
☑ Tick the best W.
☑ Tick the best Y.

Checklist
☐ U and V have no pen lifts.
☐ Y is formed by making the 'v' first, pen lift and then making the vertical line.
☐ The diagonal slopes are balanced.

Name .... Date ....

Say the sounds. Trace the letters.

X X X X   Z Z Z Z

Trace and write the letters.

X X   X

Z Z   Z

Check
☑ Tick the best X.
☑ Tick the best Z.

Checklist
☐ The right-to-left slopes on Z and X are the same angle.
☐ All lines meet at sharp points.
☐ Form X left to right and then pen lift, right to left slanting backwards.
☐ Form Z with no pen lifts.

Name .... Date ....

Trace the numbers. Say their names.

1 2 3 4 5

Trace the numbers. Think about their starting points.

1 2 3 4 5   1 2 3 4 5

Write the numbers.

_____

The number I can write best is:

The number I still need to practise is:

Name .... Date ....

Trace the numbers. Say their names.

6 7 8 9 10

Trace the numbers. Think about their starting points.

6 7 8 9 10   6 7 8 9 10

Write the numbers.

_____

The number I can write best is:

The number I still need to practise is:

Name .... Date ....

Say the words. Trace them.

lolly   yellow   Luis

Trace the words.

lolly lolly   yellow yellow   Luis Luis

Write the words.

_____   _____   _____

Check
☑ Tick the best _l_.

Checklist
- ☐ _l_ is twice the height of _o_.
- ☐ Letters end in a flick, not a curve.
- ☐ _l_s are parallel.
- ☐ Capital _L_ is formed correctly and is the same height as ascenders.

Name .... Date ....

Read the sentence. Trace it.

Luis licked his yellow lolly.

Trace the sentence.

Luis licked his yellow lolly.

Write the sentence.

_____

Check
☑ Tick the best two _l_s.

Checklist
- ☐ _l_ is twice the height of _o_.
- ☐ Letters end in a flick, not a curve.
- ☐ _l_s are parallel.
- ☐ Capital _L_ is formed correctly and is the same height as ascenders.
- ☐ Can the child write this dictated phrase: _Ling had a long list._

Name .... Date ....

Say the words. Trace them.

little   kids   river

Trace the words.

little little   kids kids   river river

Write the words.

_____   _____   _____

Check
☑ Tick the best *i*.

Checklist
☐ *i* ends in a flick, not a curve.
☐ The dot on the letter *i* is a single pencil dot.

Name .... Date ....

Read the sentence. Trace it.

Six little kids are in a river.

Trace the sentence.

Six little kids are in a river.

Write the sentence.

_____

Check
☑ Tick the best two *i*s.

Checklist
☐ *i* ends in a flick, not a curve.
☐ The dot on the letter *i* is a single pencil dot.
☐ Can the child write this dictated phrase: *Is Tim sitting in his sink?*

Name .... Date ....

Say the words. Trace them.

ten   teeth   Tim

Trace the words.

ten ten   teeth teeth   Tim Tim

Write the words.

_____ _____ _____

Check
☑ Tick the best *t*.

Checklist
☐ The bottom of the letter *t* ends in a curve, not a flick.
☐ The cross bar on *t* is the same height and width as *e*.
☐ *t* is slightly shorter than *h*.
☐ *T* is the same height as ascenders.

Name .... Date ....

Read the sentence. Trace it.

Tim had ten tiny little teeth.

Trace the sentence.

Tim had ten tiny little teeth.

Write the sentence.

_____

Check
☑ Tick the best two *t*s.

Checklist
☐ The bottom of the letter *t* ends in a curve, not a flick.
☐ The cross bar on *t* is the same height and width as *e*.
☐ *t* is slightly shorter than *h*.
☐ *T* is the same height as ascenders.
☐ Can the child write this dictated phrase: *The toy tractor turns into a train.*

Name .... Date ....

Say the words. Trace them.

Mum   upset   uncle

Trace the words.

Mum Mum   upset upset   uncle uncle

Write the words.

_____   _____   _____

Check
☑ Tick the best _u_.

Checklist
☐ The second downstroke in _u_ traces the line of the upstroke.
☐ Downstrokes and upstrokes in _u_ are equal heights.
☐ _u_ is the same height as _m_.
☐ _M_ is the same height as ascenders.

Name .... Date ....

Read the sentence. Trace it.

Mum was upset with Uncle Ull.

Trace the sentence.

Mum was upset with Uncle Ull.

Write the sentence.

_____

Check
☑ Tick the best two _u_s.

Checklist
☐ The second downstroke in _u_ traces the line of the upstroke.
☐ Downstrokes and upstrokes in _u_ are equal heights.
☐ _u_ is the same height as _m_.
☐ _M_ is the same height as ascenders.
☐ Can the child write this dictated phrase: _Yuri put his umbrella up_.

Name .... Date ....

Say the words. Trace them.

jump   joy   Jay

Trace the words.

jump jump   joy joy   Jay Jay

Write the words.

_____   _____   _____

Check
☑ Tick the best _j_.

Checklist
☐ The bottom of the letter _j_ curves to the left.
☐ Add the dot to _j_ at the end.
☐ The top of the _j_ is the same height as a letter _u_.
☐ The top of _J_ is the same height as an ascender.

Name .... Date ....

Read the sentence. Trace it.

Jay jumps for joy in July.

Trace the sentence.

Jay jumps for joy in July.

Write the sentence.

_____

Check
☑ Tick the best two _j_s.

Checklist
☐ The bottom of the letter _j_ curves to the left.
☐ Add the dot to _j_ at the end.
☐ The top of the _j_ is the same height as a letter _u_.
☐ The top of _J_ is the same height as an ascender.
☐ Can the child write this dictated phrase:
  Jen has a jar of jam in her jacket.

Name .... Date ....

Say the words. Trace them.

tiger   roar   river

Trace the words.

tiger tiger   roar roar   river river

Write the words.

_____   _____   _____

Check
☑ Tick the best *r*.

Checklist
☐ The letter *r* starts at the top.
☐ The bounce-up stroke traces the line of the downstroke.
☐ The bounce-up and over stops at about 1 o'clock.

Name .... Date ....

Read the sentence. Trace it.

Raj the tiger roars near the river.

Trace the sentence.

Raj the tiger roars near the river.

Write the sentence.

_____

Check
☑ Tick the best two *r*s.

Checklist
☐ The letter *r* starts at the top.
☐ The bounce-up stroke traces the line of the downstroke.
☐ The bounce-up and over stops at about 1 o'clock.
☐ Can the child write this dictated phrase:
The red ram runs around the room.

Name .... Date ....

Say the words. Trace them.

bun   bed   Bob

Trace the words.

bun bun   bed bed   Bob Bob

Write the words.

_____   _____   _____

Check
☑ Tick the best _b_.

Checklist
☐ The letter _b_ starts at the top.
☐ The bounce-up stroke traces the same line as the downstroke.
☐ The letter is fully closed at the bottom and finishes with a swing to the left.
☐ _B_ is the same height as ascenders.

Name .... Date ....

Read the sentence. Trace it.

Bob ate a burnt bun in bed.

Trace the sentence.

Bob ate a burnt bun in bed.

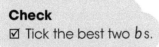

Write the sentence.

_____

Check
☑ Tick the best two _b_ s.

Checklist
☐ The letter _b_ starts at the top.
☐ The bounce-up stroke traces the same line as the downstroke.
☐ The letter is fully closed at the bottom and finishes with a swing to the left.
☐ _B_ is the same height as ascenders.
☐ Can the child write this dictated phrase:
   Bill rubbed Ben's bicycle with a black bit of cloth.

Name .... Date ....

Say the words. Trace them.

newt   nine   Nat

Trace the words.

newt newt   nine nine   Nat Nat

Write the words.

_____   _____   _____

Check
☑ Tick the best *n*.

Checklist
☐ The letter *n* starts at the top.
☐ The bounce-up stroke traces the same line as the downstroke.
☐ The downstrokes are parallel.
☐ *N* is the same height as ascenders but slightly taller than *t*.

Penpals Intervention Book 1

© Cambridge-Hitachi 2016. You may photocopy this PCM.

Name .... Date ....

Read the sentence. Trace it.

Nat needed nine new newt nets.

Trace the sentence.

Nat needed nine new newt nets.

Write the sentence.

_____

Check
☑ Tick the best two *n*s.

Checklist
☐ The letter *n* starts at the top.
☐ The bounce-up stroke traces the same line as the downstroke.
☐ The downstrokes are parallel.
☐ *N* is the same height as ascenders but slightly taller than *t*.
☐ Can the child write this dictated phrase:
    Noon is not at night.

Penpals Intervention Book 1

© Cambridge-Hitachi 2016. You may photocopy this PCM.

Name .... Date ....

Say the words. Trace them.

three   teeth   Hannah

Trace the words.

three three   teeth teeth   Hannah Hannah

Write the words.

_____   _____   _____

Check
☑ Tick the best *h*.

Checklist
☐ The letter *h* starts at the top.
☐ The downstroke is twice the height of the bounce-up.
☐ The second downstroke is parallel to the first.
☐ *H* is the same height as ascenders.

Name .... Date ....

Read the sentence. Trace it.

Hannah has three teeth.

Trace the sentence.

Hannah has three teeth.

Write the sentence.

_____

Check
☑ Tick the best two *h* s.

Checklist
☐ The letter *h* starts at the top.
☐ The downstroke is twice the height of the bounce-up.
☐ The second downstroke is parallel to the first.
☐ *H* is the same height as ascenders.
☐ Can the child write this dictated phrase: *He has hot hands.*

Name .... Date ....

Say the words. Trace them.

Mum remember

Trace the words.

Mum Mum remember remember

Write the words.

_____   _____

Check
☑ Tick the best *m*.

Checklist
☐ The letter *m* starts at the top.
☐ The bounce-up strokes trace the same line as the downstrokes.
☐ Both of the curves are the same height.
☐ *M* is the same height as ascenders.

Name .... Date ....

Read the sentence. Trace it.

Mum remembers swimming.

Trace the sentence.

Mum remembers swimming.

Write the sentence.

_____

Check
☑ Tick the best two *m*s.

Checklist
☐ The letter *m* starts at the top.
☐ The bounce-up strokes trace the same line as the downstrokes.
☐ Both of the curves are the same height.
☐ *M* is the same height as ascenders.
☐ Can the child write this dictated phrase:
   My mum makes yummy marshmallows.

Name .... Date ....

Say the words. Trace them.

kitten   black   Kate

Trace the words.

kitten kitten   black black   Kate Kate

Write the words.

_____   _____   _____

Check
☑ Tick the best _k_.

Checklist
☐ The long _k_ downstroke is twice the height of the bounce-up.
☐ The end of the hoop touches the long downstroke.
☐ The hoop and the final diagonal are the same distance from the downstroke.
☐ _K_ is the same height as ascenders.

Unit 40b: Sentences with _k_

Name .... Date ....

Read the sentence. Trace it.

Kate's black kitten had a drink.

Trace the sentence.

Kate's black kitten had a drink.

Write the sentence.

_____

Check
☑ Tick the best two _k_ s.

Checklist
☐ The long _k_ downstroke is twice the height of the bounce-up.
☐ The end of the hoop touches the long downstroke.
☐ The hoop and the final diagonal are the same distance from the downstroke.
☐ _K_ is the same height as ascenders.
☐ Can the child write this dictated phrase: _King Kevin kept a kangaroo._

Name ....   Date ....

Say the words. Trace them.

puppy   paw   Paul

Trace the words.

puppy puppy   paw paw   Paul Paul

Write the words.

_____   _____   _____

Check
☑ Tick the best *p*.

Checklist
☐ The letter *p* starts at the top of the downstroke.
☐ The bounce-up traces the same line as the downstroke.
☐ The curve finishes by touching the downstroke and rests on the baseline.
☐ *P* is the same height as ascenders.

Unit 41b: Sentences with *p*

Name ....   Date ....

Read the sentence. Trace it.

Paul's puppy has padded paws.

Trace the sentence.

Paul's puppy has padded paws.

Write the sentence.

_____

Check
☑ Tick the best two *p* s.

Checklist
☐ The letter *p* starts at the top of the downstroke.
☐ The bounce-up traces the same line as the downstroke
☐ The curve finishes by touching the downstroke and rests on the baseline.
☐ *P* is the same height as ascenders.
☐ Can the child write this dictated phrase: *Pete picked up a pizza for the picnic in the park.*

Name .... Date ....

Say the words. Trace them.

cook   crab   Carl

Trace the words.

cook cook   crab crab   Carl Carl

Write the words.

_____   _____   _____

Check
☑ Tick the best c.

Checklist
☐ The letter c starts at 1 o'clock.
☐ The curve at the top of the letter matches the curve at the bottom of the letter.
☐ C is the same height as ascenders.

Name .... Date ....

Read the sentence. Trace it.

Can Carl cook a rock crab?

Trace the sentence.

Can Carl cook a rock crab?

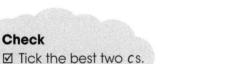

Write the sentence.

_____

Check
☑ Tick the best two cs.

Checklist
☐ The letter c starts at 1 o'clock.
☐ The curve at the top of the letter matches the curve at the bottom of the letter.
☐ C is the same height as ascenders.
☐ Can the child write this dictated phrase:
   Can the cat get a cap?

Name .... Date ....

Say the words. Trace them.

cat   bag   Anna

Trace the words.

cat cat   bag bag   Anna Anna

Write the words.

_____   _____   _____

Check
☑ Tick the best *a*.

Checklist
☐ The letter *a* starts at 1 o'clock.
☐ The letter is fully closed at the top.
☐ The downstroke traces the line of the upstroke.
☐ *A* is the same height as ascenders.

Penpals Intervention Book 1

Name .... Date ....

Read the sentence. Trace it.

Anna has a cat in a black bag.

Trace the sentence.

Anna has a cat in a black bag.

Write the sentence.

_____

Check
☑ Tick the best two *a*s.

Checklist
☐ The letter *a* starts at 1 o'clock.
☐ The letter is fully closed at the top.
☐ The downstroke traces the line of the upstroke.
☐ *A* is the same height as ascenders.
☐ Can the child write this dictated phrase:
   A man in a cap sat in a van.

Penpals Intervention Book 1

Name _____ Date _____

Say the words. Trace them.

doll   drop   Dad

Trace the words.

doll doll   drop drop   Dad Dad

Write the words.

_____ _____ _____

Check
☑ Tick the best *d*.

Checklist
☐ The letter *d* starts at 1 o'clock at the top of the curve.
☐ The curve is joined to the downstroke.
☐ The downstroke traces the line of the upstroke.
☐ *D* is the same height as ascenders.

Name _____ Date _____

Read the sentence. Trace it.

Did Dad drop Daisy's doll?

Trace the sentence.

Did Dad drop Daisy's doll?

Write the sentence.

_____

Check
☑ Tick the best two *d*s.

Checklist
☐ The letter *d* starts at 1 o'clock at the top of the curve.
☐ The curve is joined to the downstroke.
☐ The downstroke traces the line of the upstroke.
☐ *D* is the same height as ascenders.
☐ Can the child write this dictated phrase: *Dan had a bad dog*.

Name .... Date ....

Say the words. Trace them.

frog   *hop*   *One*

Trace the words.

frog frog   *hop hop*   *one one*

Write the words.

_____   _____   _____

Check
☑ Tick the best *o*.

Checklist
☐ The letter *o* starts at 1 o'clock.
☐ The letter is formed anticlockwise.
☐ The letter begins and ends at the same place.
☐ *O* is the same height as ascenders.

Name .... Date ....

Read the sentence. Trace it.

One frog hopped off the old log.

Trace the sentence.

One frog hopped off the old log.

Write the sentence.

_____

Check
☑ Tick the best two *o*s.

Checklist
☐ The letter *o* starts at 1 o'clock.
☐ The letter is formed anticlockwise.
☐ The letter begins and ends at the same place.
☐ *O* is the same height as ascenders.
☐ Can the child write this dictated phrase:
   Open the box for the dog to hop on.

Name .... Date ....

Say the words. Trace them.

stripy   scissors   handles

Trace the words.

stripy stripy   scissors scissors   handles handles

Write the words.

_____   _____   _____

Check
☑ Tick the best *s*.

Checklist
☐ The letter *s* begins with a curve.
☐ The curves are balanced.
☐ The letter is the same height as a *c*.

Penpals Intervention Book 1
© Cambridge-Hitachi 2016. You may photocopy this PCM.

Name .... Date ....

Read the sentence. Trace it.

Sam's scissors have stripy handles.

Trace the sentence.

Sam's scissors have stripy handles.

Write the sentence.

_____

Check
☑ Tick the best two *s* s.

Checklist
☐ The letter *s* begins with a curve.
☐ The curves are balanced.
☐ The letter is the same height as a *c*.
☐ *S* is the same height as ascenders.
☐ Can the child write this dictated phrase:
Sally saw seven stars in the sky.

Penpals Intervention Book 1
© Cambridge-Hitachi 2016. You may photocopy this PCM.

Name .... Date ....

Say the words. Trace them.

goat   green   George

Trace the words.

goat goat   green green   George George

Write the words.

....

Check

☑ Tick the best _g_.

Name .... Date ....

Read the sentence. Trace it.

George's goat is bright green.

Trace the sentence.

George's goat is bright green.

Write the sentence.

....

Check

☑ Tick the best two _g_ s.

Name .... Date ....

Say the words. Trace them.

queen   queue   quiet

Trace the words.

queen queen   queue queue   quiet quiet

Write the words.

_____   _____   _____

Check
☑ Tick the best q.

Checklist
☐ The letter q starts at 1 o'clock.
☐ The top of the downstroke touches the starting point to close the letter.
☐ The flick goes up towards the baseline.

Name .... Date ....

Read the sentence. Trace it.

The queen queued quite quietly.

Trace the sentence.

The queen queued quite quietly.

Write the sentence.

_____

Check
☑ Tick the best two q s.

Checklist
☐ The letter q starts at 1 o'clock.
☐ The top of the downstroke touches the starting point to close the letter.
☐ The flick goes up towards the baseline.
☐ Can the child write this dictated phrase:
"Quick, quick!" the duck quacked.

Name ....   Date ....

Say the words. Trace them.

hen   egg   red

Trace the words.

hen hen   egg egg   red red

Write the words.

_____   _____   _____

Check
☑ Tick the best *e*.

Checklist
☐ The letter *e* begins with a gentle curve from left to right.
☐ The starting point and downward curve should touch.
☐ The curve at the bottom matches that at the top.

Name ....   Date ....

Read the sentence. Trace it.

Emma held the hen's new egg.

Trace the sentence.

Emma held the hen's new egg.

Write the sentence.

_____

Check
☑ Tick the best two *e*s.

Checklist
☐ The letter *e* begins with a gentle curve from left to right.
☐ The starting point and downward curve should touch.
☐ The curve at the bottom matches that at the top.
☐ *E* is the same height as ascenders.
☐ Can the child write this dictated phrase:
  Ben can get the red pens.

Name .... Date ....

Say the words. Trace them.

fifty-four   fish   Fifi

Trace the words.

fifty-four fifty-four   fish fish   Fifi Fifi

Write the words.

_____   _____   _____

Check
☑ Tick the best *f*.

Checklist
☐ The letter *f* starts as a curve from 1 o'clock.
☐ The downstroke is parallel with those in other letters.
☐ The top and bottom curves are similar sizes.
☐ Letter *f* needs a vertical line - it's not a long *s*.
☐ *F* is the same height as ascenders.

- -

Name .... Date ....

Read the sentence. Trace it.

Fifi found fifty-four fish.

Trace the sentence.

Fifi found fifty-four fish.

Write the sentence.

_____

Check
☑ Tick the best two *f*s.

Checklist
☐ The letter *f* starts as a curve from 1 o'clock.
☐ The letter slopes slightly forward.
☐ The top and bottom curves are similar sizes.
☐ *F* is the same height as ascenders.
☐ Can the child write this dictated phrase:
  Fred has fun with a frog in the fog.

Unit 51a: Words with *v*, *w* and *x*

Name _____ Date _____

Say the words. Trace them.

wet white six vixen

Trace the words.

wet wet *white white* *six six* *vixen vixen*

Write the words.

_____ _____ _____ _____

Check
☑ Tick the best *v*.
☑ Tick the best *w*.
☑ Tick the best *x*.

Checklist
☐ All diagonal downstrokes and upstrokes in *w* and *x* are the same height.
☐ The cross of *x* is at, or slightly above, the midpoint.
☐ The 'v's in the *w* are balanced.

Unit 51b: Sentences with *v*, *w* and *x*

Name _____ Date _____

Read the sentence. Trace it.

Six wet foxes saw a white vixen.

Trace the sentence.

Six wet foxes saw a white vixen.

Write the sentence.

_____

Check
☑ Tick the best *v*.
☑ Tick the best two *w*s.
☑ Tick the best two *x*s.

Checklist
☐ All diagonal downstrokes and upstrokes in *w* and *x* are the same height.
☐ The cross of *x* is at, or slightly above, the midpoint.
☐ The 'v's in the *w* are balanced.
☐ Can the child write this dictated phrase:
  We have wax in the white box.

Name .... Date ....

Say the words. Trace them.

yellow   zebra   zoo

Trace the words.

yellow yellow   zebra zebra   zoo zoo

Write the words.

_____ _____ _____

Check
☑ Tick the best y.
☑ Tick the best z.

Checklist
☐ y and z are the same width.
☐ z is the same height as a.
☐ The length of the descender of the y matches the height above the line.

Name .... Date ....

Read the sentence. Trace it.

Your yellow zebra is in the zoo.

Trace the sentence.

Your yellow zebra is in the zoo.

Write the sentence.

_____

Check
☑ Tick the best two ys.
☑ Tick the best two zs.

Checklist
☐ y and z are the same width.
☐ z is the same height as a.
☐ The length of the descender of the y matches the height above the line.
☐ Y is the same height as ascenders.
☐ Can the child write this dictated phrase:
    Did the yellow bees buzz at you?